THE FOLGER
SHAKESPEARE
LIBRARY

WASHINGTON

THE FOLGER SHAKESPEARE LIBRARY

WASHINGTON

PUBLISHED FOR

THE TRUSTEES OF AMHERST COLLEGE

1933

The photographs in this book are the work of Messrs. Horydczak, of Washington, Rittase, of Philadelphia, and Gottscho, of New York. Reproduced in Full-tone collotype by The Meriden Gravure Co., Meriden, Conn., U.S.A.

FOREWORD

By the *bequest of the late Henry Clay Folger the ownership in trust of the Folger Shakespeare Library in Washington is vested in the Trustees of Amherst College. The trust involves a three-fold responsibility: first, for the proper care and use of the large collection of books, manuscripts, objects of art, and memorabilia relating to Shakespeare and the Elizabethan Age; secondly, for the maintenance of the Library building; and, thirdly, for the management of the funds provided under the terms of Mr. Folger's will as an endowment for the Library, and later generously increased by Mrs. Folger.*

It was Mr. Folger's expressed intention that his gift should be used for the advancement of literary study in the United States. With this object in view he determined that the Folger Library should be permanently located in the nation's Capital, where the resources of the Library of Congress would also be available to readers, and that its administration should be entrusted to the governing board of an institution of higher learning. His selection of the Trustees of Amherst College followed naturally from his early association with the college, where he was graduated in the class of 1879, and from his intimate connection in business with Amherst men. In recognition of the part that Amherst had played in developing his own love of fine literature, he looked confidently to its Board of Trustees to perpetuate his lifework as a Shakespearian scholar and collector.

The career of Henry Clay Folger is not less remarkable for his success in the management of a great industrial enterprise than for his achievement in forming a Shakespeare library unmatched by any existing

[vii]

collection. *Born in New York City on June 18, 1857, he prepared for college at Adelphi Academy, where he was the holder of a scholarship donated by Mr. Charles Pratt, then president of the Academy trustees. He entered Amherst College in the same class with Mr. Pratt's eldest son, Charles M. Pratt, with whom he became a member of the Alpha Delta Phi fraternity. In college Mr. Folger was keenly interested in English composition and oratory, winning prizes in both subjects in the face of strenuous competition. He also received a first appointment to Phi Beta Kappa. After graduation he entered as a clerk the office of Charles Pratt, and at the same time studied law at Columbia College, from which institution he received the degree of LL.B., cum laude, in 1881. He thereafter gave his undivided attention to business. As his abilities were tested and developed he steadily rose to positions of greater responsibility. In June, 1908, he was elected to the board of the Standard Oil Company of New Jersey, and shortly afterward was made a member of the executive committee; in February, 1909, he was also elected a director of the Standard Oil Company of New York. After the dissolution of 1911, in which Mr. Folger played a part second only in importance to that of John D. Rockefeller, he accepted the presidency of the New York Company and continued in that office until May, 1923, when he was made chairman of the board. He remained the chief executive officer of the Company until his retirement five years later. In the short interval left him before his death on June 11, 1930, he devoted himself entirely to his Shakespeare library and the construction of the building designed to house it.*

During all his years as a responsible executive Mr. Folger cultivated the delight in good reading that was his native endowment, though intensified by his college training and strongly stimulated by Emerson, whom he heard lecture at Amherst in the spring of his senior year. His special interest in Shakespeariana was an outgrowth of his study of the dramatist's works in a facsimile reproduction of the First Folio. With increasingly ample means at his disposal, he proceeded quietly to form his library as opportunities offered, not without sharp competition with Henry E. Huntington and other ardent book-collectors. His single-minded concentration on Shakespeare, however, was an advantage to him: he came to be known to dealers as the principal collector of Shakespeariana, and in consequence he was usually first offered whatever rarities came upon the market. By 1914 his library had become so notable that he was awarded the degree of Doctor of Letters by his Alma Mater; and long before his death it surpassed any Shakespeare collection ever brought together. For one man to outdo the labors of generations of collectors was a unique achievement; Mr. Folger accomplished this feat by intense concentration during his few daily hours of leisure.

In the work of book-collecting Mr. Folger's interest was completely shared by his wife, formerly Emily C. Jordan, whom he married on October 6, 1885. Mrs. Folger, a graduate and a Master of Arts of Vassar College, became his eager assistant, entering into every phase of his plans, and tirelessly keeping records of the items purchased. Both felt themselves consecrated to the same ideal. After Mr. Folger's death, Mrs. Folger was able to see his intentions in regard to the Library fulfilled, and in 1932 she, like him, was awarded the degree of Doctor of Letters by Amherst College.

The Trustees of Amherst received notice of their administrative responsibility for the Folger Shakespeare Library when the building was in process of construction. It remained for them, with Mrs. Folger's assistance, to complete the building, select the staff, and arrange for the installation of the books, which were in safety deposit vaults and warehouses in New York and Brooklyn. By the spring of 1932 this part of the work had been accomplished. In the presence of Mrs. Folger, President and Mrs. Hoover, and a notable gathering of statesmen, educators, and scholars, the Folger Shakespeare Library was formally dedicated on April 23, the three hundred and sixty-eighth anniversary of Shakespeare's birth. After the exercises of dedication, the building was thrown open to public inspection. By the following autumn the preliminary work of arranging and tentatively cataloguing the books and manuscripts had so far progressed that the Reading Room was opened to qualified students. The full development of the resources of the collections, however, cannot be completed for some years to come.

The administration of the Library is carried on by a committee of eight members of the Board of Trustees of Amherst College, of which the President of the Board and the President of the College are members ex officio. The President of the College is also the executive officer of the committee. The executive officer of the Library is the Director; matters of research are in charge of the Supervisor of Research. That part of the building containing the Exhibition Hall and the Theater is open to public inspection on week days.

TRUSTEES OF AMHERST COLLEGE

HARLAN FISKE STONE,
*Chairman of the Committee
on the Folger Shakespeare Library*

WILLIAM ADAMS SLADE,
Director of the Library

[x]

THE LIBRARY

BY

JOSEPH QUINCY ADAMS

THE LIBRARY

MR. FOLGER'S love for works of the imagination, the ultimate centering of his affection upon Shakespeare, and the devotion of his life to assembling material about his chosen master, may here fittingly be sketched by way of introduction to our topic.

As an undergraduate at Amherst, 1875-79, when the emphasis of the curriculum was on the ancient classics and mathematics, Mr. Folger showed a pronounced interest in English literature. With an essay on Charles Dickens he won, in his Junior year, the Prize in Composition, and with an oration on Alfred Tennyson he won, in his Senior year, the coveted Prize in Public Speaking. Though at first, as these two episodes would suggest, his main bent was toward our modern rather than our earlier writers, he must have held Shakespeare in esteem; we know, for instance, that he joined a club of students organized for the purpose of reading the plays aloud. What, then, served to focus his interest on the remote dramatist of the Elizabethan age? The answer to that question will furnish an insight into his character. In his Senior year at college he attended—though few of his fellow students availed themselves of the opportunity—a lecture by Ralph Waldo Emerson on "Superlative or Mental Temperance"; and so profoundly did the beautiful English and flaming intellect of the speaker inspire him that when, shortly after, he came upon an excerpt from an address which Emerson had made in 1864 before the Saturday Club of Boston, on the Tercentenary of Shakespeare's birth, he read it with avidity. Emerson's glowing eulogy of Shakespeare as the world's outstanding genius fired young Folger's imagination, and sent him at once to a thorough study of the works of the great master. In spite of straitened means, he purchased Routledge's "Handy-Volume" edition of the poet in thirteen small volumes, which, so he confided to one of his friends, he was accustomed to read, after his scholastic duties were over, "far into the night." Mrs. Folger states that her husband's chance discovery of the Saturday Club address by Emerson constitutes the real beginning of his passionate devotion to Shakespeare. We can therefore understand why, when he came to plan the Library, he ordered to be carved over the large fireplace in the Reading Room lines from Emerson embodying the thought of that address; and why, when the building was dedicated, the address itself was read to the assembled guests.

Mr. Folger thus left Amherst endowed with a profound and quickening love for Shakespeare, a precious heritage that was to enrich the rest of his life.

Upon graduation he began to study law, supporting himself meanwhile by serving as a part-time clerk in the office of Charles Pratt and Company, oil refiners associated with the Standard Oil group. Two years later, in 1881, he received from Columbia College the degree of LL.B., *cum laude,* and was formally admitted to the New York bar. Charles Pratt and Company thereupon offered him a permanent connection with its organization; and, after some hesitation, he finally decided to forgo a professional and seek a business career in the rapidly developing petroleum industry. For him the decision was momentous, in that it led him to notable success as an executive, to the Presidency of the Standard Oil Company, and to a great personal fortune.

But fate, though it thrust him into the active leadership of one of America's greatest industries, was not to let him lose his interest in Shakespeare. On the contrary, that interest was soon to be accentuated. In 1885 he married Emily Clara Jordan, who, as an undergraduate at Vassar, and subsequently as a teacher of literature, had developed an ardent admiration for the poet; and her sympathy did much to further his enthusiastic study of the plays. A few months after marriage, he purchased for $1.25 a copy of Halliwell-Phillipps' reduced facsimile of the First Folio, and brought it home to his wife with the remark: "Here you may see Shakespeare's plays as they were actually given to the world." Mrs. Folger is accustomed to refer to this volume as "the cornerstone of the Shakespeare Library"; for an examination of it led Mr. Folger to become deeply interested in the fascinating matter of first editions, the mystery of the quarto and folio texts, and, finally, the whole field of Shakespearian scholarship. So profoundly, indeed, did the volume influence him that years later he eagerly seized the opportunity to purchase the very copy of the First Folio that Halliwell-Phillipps had used for his reproduction; moreover, it became his custom to buy all copies of reduced facsimiles he saw offered for sale, and to present one as a graduation gift to every young student dear to him.

His newly aroused interest in the early text of Shakespeare's plays soon found expression in a way that, quite unsuspected by him, was to determine the future course of his life. In 1889 a copy of the Fourth Folio (1685) was advertised for sale at Bangs' auction-room in New York City, and Mr. Folger, though still relatively a poor man, was tempted to make a try for it. "With fear and trepidation," as he expressed it—fear at his proposed extravagance, trepidation at a strange experience—he entered the auction-room, and, following up each competing bid with a small increment, finally saw the coveted volume knocked down to him for $107.50. Not finding it convenient to pay at once, he asked and received credit for thirty days. When, at the end of a month, he had settled in full for the volume, he proudly possessed his first Shakespearian rarity; and he had irrevocably launched himself upon the entrancing sea of collecting. From now on, the bringing together of material relating to the poet and his age became the chief passion of his life.

In 1899, in an account of his activities contributed to his College Class History, he wrote: "The gathering of a modest library has helped to keep me interested in matters literary." As his income steadily increased, he extended his buying to include ever rarer books, and, occasionally, manuscripts; so that five years later, in 1904, for the same Class History, he wrote: "I have made a collection of material illustrating Shakespeare, which, I believe, will soon be notable." His purchases keeping steady pace with the growth of his fortune, five years later, in 1909, he was able to inform his classmates: "I have found the means for adding to my collection of Shakespeariana, until it is perhaps the largest and finest in America, and perhaps in the world." With excusable pride he added: "That is really saying a great deal." It was, indeed; yet for twenty-one years longer, with unabated enthusiasm, he continued to add to his store of treasures, until, in 1932, Dr. Rosenbach, without any qualifying "perhaps," declared it to be "the finest collection of Shakespeariana that the world has known."

By nature shy and retiring, Mr. Folger found in the task of assembling his great library a happy expression of his inner self. Outside his business hours, he lived with and in his books and manuscripts, taking his main joy in searching the catalogues of dealers, daring the battles of the auction-room, and, with the satisfaction of a creative artist, rounding his collection into full perfection. His nephew, Mr. Dimock, writes: "The singularity of his life's purpose made interchange of confidence with his fellows supremely difficult, and his reticence led to an intellectual loneliness which would doubtless have been insupportable had it been absolute." Fortunately it was not absolute. In his wife he found complete understanding and sympathy—complete co-operation, too; and hand in hand they marched through the long-stretching years, as on a grand adventure, searching for and joyfully bringing together precious material about the poet they both loved. In the fullest sense of the word they were "collaborators," sharing with each other the infinite pain, and the no less infinite pleasure, known only to the collector. It is thus fitting that in the Reading Room of the finished Library their portairts—companion studies by the artist Salisbury—hang side by side, looking down upon the fruits of their joint labor.

As their collection began to assume unique importance, Mr. and Mrs. Folger conceived the idea of leaving it as a gift to the American people, beautifully housed and adequately endowed for upkeep and growth. Having decided to place it in the nation's Capital, Mr. Folger visited Washington, and, through a series of quiet negotiations extended over nine years, purchased fourteen separate parcels of land constituting half a city block adjoining the Library of Congress. With the purchase of the site achieved, he next engaged architects to design a suitable building; and in June, 1930, he had the satisfaction of knowing that the cornerstone had been laid. Two weeks later he died. But his wife carried on the work he left unfinished; and on April 23, 1932, presented the keys of the completed Library, with all the collections assembled, to the Trustees of Amherst College, who thereby assumed, under the terms of Mr. Folger's will, the responsibility of administering it for ever as an educational institution "for the promotion and diffusion of knowledge in regard to the history and writings of Shakespeare."

The first impression that one gains upon examining the material housed in the Library is of its "infinite variety." Here, in almost unbelievable fulness and richness, are assembled books, pamphlets, documents, manuscripts, relics, curios, oil-paintings, original drawings, water colors, prints, statues, busts, medals, coins, miscellaneous objects of art, furniture, tapestries, playbills, prompt-books, stage-properties, actors' costumes, and other material designed to illustrate the poet and his times. The Library is thus more than a mere library; it is also a museum of the Golden Age of Elizabeth, and a memorial to the influence that Shakespeare has exerted upon the world's culture.

Since Mr. Folger's impulse to collect was originally inspired by Halliwell-Phillipps' facsimile of the First Folio, it is natural that he should bring together early editions of the poet. Of the First Folio, 1623, though only about two hundred examples are known to exist, the Library possesses no fewer than seventy-nine. In addition, it has the texts of the individual plays extracted from imperfect copies of the Folio, in three or four examples of each, so that it would be possible to assemble from these excerpts at least two virtually complete First Folios, and a generous fragment of a third. This astonishing collection—the largest number of First Folios in any other Library, the British Museum, is five

—is further enriched by: two examples of the Droeshout portrait engraving in the proof state, including a unique impression of the title-page in its first state; a page with corrections by the original proof-reader; the copy of the Folio presented by its publisher, William Jaggard, to his friend Augustine Vincent, one of the earliest copies to come from the press, the largest copy known, partly in its original binding, and fondly described by Mr. Folger as "the most precious book in the world"; the copy bearing the signature of the Elizabethan player, Samuel Gilburne, whose name stands in the list of "The Principall Actors in all these Playes"; and numerous copies with canceled or duplicate leaves, and important variant readings. Of the Second Folio, 1632, the Library possesses fifty-eight examples, including copies that belonged to Elizabeth, only daughter of King James I (whose marriage in 1613 was celebrated with performances by Shakespeare's troupe of eight of the master's plays, some of which he is thought to have revised for the occasion), David Garrick, George Colman (with autograph verses), Lewis Theobald (with his manuscript annotations), William Pitt, Earl of Chatham, Horace Walpole, and Samuel Johnson (with elaborate notes); of the Third Folio, 1664, twenty-four examples, including, besides every variation of imprint, a copy said to be Alexander Pope's, used by him for his great edition, and filled with manuscript annotations; of the Fourth Folio, 1685, thirty-six examples (in addition to various fragments), including the two largest copies known, and copies that belonged to Edmund Kean, Charles Matthews, David Garrick, Sarah Siddons, George Eliot, John Ruskin, Edward Fitzgerald, and William Morris. In all, the Library houses approximately two hundred Folios— a collection that in numbers and in richness is not elsewhere remotely approached, and that can never be equaled.

Of the attempted "collection" of Shakespeare's plays made by Thomas Pavier in 1619, the Library has the only two copies known; one, the Gwynn, is complete, and in its original binding, the other, formerly the property of Bishop Percy, lacks two of the plays, which, as the good Bishop notes on the flyleaf, he removed from the volume as gifts to friends. It is remarkable that still a third complete copy of the 1619 collection is in the Library, though a previous owner has taken the plays apart and had each separately bound.

The individual editions of the plays in quarto have, of course, not been neglected; on the contrary, to quote no less an authority than Dr. Rosenbach, the Library possesses "the greatest number of Shakespearian quartos ever gathered." The gem of the collection is, perhaps, the unique copy of the first edition of *Titus Andronicus*, 1594, the earliest of the dramatist's published plays, in immaculate condition. A few other treasures may be briefly mentioned: a unique fragment of the first edition of *I Henry IV*; the 1604 edition of *Hamlet*—the first printing of the true Shakespearian text—of which only two other copies are known; a rare variant of the first edition of *King Lear*, 1608, of which only one other copy is known; three copies of the first edition of *Pericles*, 1609, one in its original paper wrappers, and the edition of 1611, of which only one other copy is known; and the 1598 edition of *Richard II*, until recently thought to be unique.

Equally notable is the collection of Shakespeare's non-dramatic works. *Venus and Adonis* is represented by the editions of 1595 (in a unique variation), 1599, 1636, and 1675 (two examples); *Lucrece*, by three copies of the first edition, 1594 (one "the finest known"), and copies of the editions of 1600, 1624 (two examples), 1632, 1636 (only one other known), and 1655 (three examples); the *Sonnets*, by two copies of the first edition, 1609; the *Poems*, by ten copies of the first edition, 1640, including one uncut, one in the original binding, and one with a "unique portrait, said to be the earliest"; *The Passionate Pilgrim*, by the first edition, 1599, of which only two other copies are known, and the third edition, 1612 (no copy of the second edition is extant), of which only one other copy is known; and *Love's Martyr* (to which Shakespeare contributed a poem), by the first edition, 1601, of which only one other copy is known.

Of early manuscripts relating to Shakespeare Mr. Folger gathered a collection that in extent and value admits no superior. Indeed, Mr.

Seymour de Ricci, after cataloguing the items before the year 1625, declares that, in the field of manuscript Shakespeariana, "the Folger Library stands out supreme." None of Shakespeare's works is extant in the handwriting of the author; but, as de Ricci observes, the Library "contains *all* the extant manuscripts of any portions of his works," including the only play in a manuscript contemporary with the poet, a version of *Henry IV* prepared about the year 1611, for use, it seems, at Court or at some private house. Of Shakespeare's signatures, all of unquestionable authenticity are attached to legal documents preserved in official archives where suspicion of forgery can not be entertained; the Library, however, has a number of attributed signatures, one or two of which may be genuine. It has also various documents—such as the four successive titles to Shakespeare's home, the purchase-deed of his Blackfriars property, and the two indentures of a fine on New Place— which were once in the poet's possession. But, in the limited scope of this essay, it is impossible to particularize, or even in general terms give an adequate conception of the extent and variety of the manuscripts assembled by Mr. Folger through forty years of industrious collecting. There are letters or documents signed by most of the persons closely associated with Shakespeare, or famous in his day, and of persons celebrated in his plays; autographs of Elizabethan actors, dramatists, and men of letters; manuscripts of literary works by contemporary writers; Tudor-Stuart plays some in the form of original prompt-books; early theatrical records; commonplace-books containing verses by eminent poet; diaries, journals, and accounts (including the Diary of the Reverend John Ward, Vicar of Stratford), and a vast number of other items bearing directly or indirectly on the poet.

Of portraits of Shakespeare, mention has already been made of the two copies of the Droeshout engraving in proof-state (of which Mr. M. H. Spielmann writes: "Not elsewhere, it may be believed, do we come so close to the living Man of Stratford"), and the unique engraved portrait prefixed to the 1640 edition of the *Poems*. The Library has also several copies of Marshall's portrait print, 1640, and four copies of

Faithorne's beautiful portrait print, 1655, so rare that, according to Spielmann, "only five impressions are known to exist." In addition, Mr. Folger acquired many early oil-portraits of the dramatist, among which the more famous are: the Felton (bearing the inscription "Gul. Shakspear, 1597, R.B.," attributed to Burbage, and regarded by Steevens as the original of the Droeshout engraving); the Kneller (formerly the property of John Dryden, who rapturously apostrophized it in verse); the Janssen ("Æ 46, 1610"); the Peele copy of the Janssen; the Ashbourne ("Ætatis suæ 47, 1611"); the Lumley (from the Burdett-Coutts collection); the "Burbage"; the Zuccaro (from the Burdett-Coutts collection); the Cosway; the Dexter; the Buttery; the Zoust; and the Gunther. With this varied assemblage of portraits should be mentioned the collection of personal relics, consisting of such items as a Stratford jury-list including the name of the dramatist's father, John; a unique impression from the seal ring of John Shakespeare; a document signed by Heminge, the manager of the Globe company of actors, carrying out certain details of the poet's will; autographs of members of his family; several pieces of wood from the birth room in Henley Street; furniture from the Birthplace and from Anne Hathaway's Cottage; a stained-glass window-pane supposed to be from Shakespeare's home, New Place; boxes, drinking-cups, statuettes, and miscellaneous objects fabricated from the Mulberry Tree, the Crab Tree, and Hearne's Oak; and scores of other more or less authentic relics that seem to bring us sentimentally closer to the man Shakespeare, who, as Heywood reminds us, to his relatives and friends "was but 'Will'."

Of Source-Books—works that Shakespeare is known to have used in the composition of his plays and poems—Mr. Folger assembled a virtually complete collection. All the ordinary items, as Painter, Holinshed, Plutarch, and the like, are, of course, fully and beautifully represented; the bibliophile, however, will find his greatest delight in such superlative rarities as Lodge's *Rosalynd* (dramatized as *As You Like It*), 1590, only one other copy known; Greene's *Pandosto* (dramatized as *Winter's Tale*), 1592, unique; *The True Tragedy of Richard III* (the source of

Shakespeare's *Richard III*), 1594, of which only two other copies are known; and, not to extend the list, Marlowe's *Hero and Leander* (from which Shakespeare directly quoted), the only extant copy of the first edition, 1598, in magnificent condition, as fresh and clean as on the day it was issued.

Of Allusion-Books—books in which Shakespeare or his plays are directly or indirectly referred to or quoted—the Library's collection is perhaps even more remarkable. Showing as they do the poet's early fame, such works had for Mr. Folger a special appeal, and he made an almost completely successful effort to bring together all that were printed before the year 1700. His private check-list—which he kept ever at his elbow—of those he had secured records more than five thousand items, many of the utmost rarity, and many unnoted by scholars; for instance, Robert Greene's *Groatsworth of Witte,* 1592 (the only other copy is in the British Museum), containing our first notice of the poet in London, the famous reference to Shakespeare as an "upstart crow"; and Thomas Middleton's *The Ghost of Lucrece,* 1600, inspired by Shakespeare's *Lucrece,* unique, hitherto unknown, and still un-reprinted. Besides allusion-books proper, Mr. Folger gathered hundreds of early manuscripts—letters, journals, commonplace-books, diaries, heraldic documents, marginally annotated volumes, etc.—containing references to the dramatist. One is irresistibly tempted to mention an unknown heraldic sketch of Shakespeare's coat of arms, and an unrecorded marginal note by Gabriel Harvey on *Richard III* and *Hamlet.*

"Shakespeare and Music" made up still another category that strongly appealed to Mr. Folger, himself a musician of ability and a generous patron of the art. As a result, the Library is richly provided with material for a study of this important subject. It has a set of Elizabethan musical instruments (originally brought together by Arnold Dolmetsch), numerous early treatises on musical theory and practice, and a large collection of vocal and instrumental music, in both printed and manuscript form. Its song-books, by Morley (including the unique *First Booke of Ayres,* 1600, with the original setting of Shakespeare's "It was a lover and his lass"), Dowland, Watson, Kirbye, Jones, Weelkes, Bennet, Wilbye, East, Ravenscroft, Yong, Byrd, and other Elizabethan composers, would render any library distinguished. Among its manuscripts is a folio volume of instrumental music for the lute, transcribed by and from the library of John Dowland (whose "heavenly touch upon the lute" is celebrated in a beautiful sonnet long attributed to Shakespeare), with Dowland's autograph in various places, and containing several tunes mentioned by the dramatist; and a love-song by Robert Jones, with the music-score and the words in the hand of Jones, and bearing at the end his signature. Of later works classified under the heading "Shakespeare and Music," a hurried count reveals approximately seven hundred titles.

As the preceding paragraph shows, Mr. Folger, in his effort to illustrate Shakespeare, did not confine his buying within narrow limits. In order to set the poet against a full background, he extended his interests to include all men of letters, both dramatic and non-dramatic, who made up what is sometimes loosely called "The Elizabethan Age," or the period stretching from the beginning of the Renaissance in England to the Commonwealth. In the field of the drama, the predecessors, contemporaries, and successors of the master are generously represented, some by unsurpassed collections; for example, the Ben Jonson collection, said to be the finest in existence. In the field of non-dramatic literature, all the important works, from the *Utopia* to *Paradise Lost*, are represented in first or extremely rare editions. The Spenser collection, with most of the first editions, John Evelyn's copy of *The Faerie Queene*, and two volumes of poems from Spenser's library, one with his autograph signature "Immerito," is notable; the Bacon collection, including the separate collections formed by Smedley and Broadbent, is easily "the most extensive and valuable ever gathered." Thus the Library in its broad scope embraces the whole period of Tudor-Stuart literature.

Nor is that all. With equal energy Mr. Folger assembled material to illuminate the thought, life, and secular history of the age. Most of the important works bearing on law, religion, politics, medicine, geography, travel, education, scholarship, psychology, the natural sciences, and like topics, he purchased in the belief that they rightly had a place in a comprehensive Shakespeare library; and these printed books he supplemented with approximately a thousand manuscripts. Among the manuscripts, those relating to the history of the period—including more than seventy letters or documents bearing the signature of Queen Elizabeth, upwards of fifty original Privy Council letters, and several hundred documents signed by the leading statesmen of the day—are of outstanding value. Mr. de Ricci states that "it will henceforth be impossible to attempt any serious work" on English history of the sixteenth and seventeenth centuries "without appealing to the resources of the Folger Library." Other groups of manuscripts—for instance, that relating to heraldry—are of prime importance. And it is only in keeping with Mr. Folger's thoroughness that he sought further to illustrate the life of the time by purchasing Elizabethan household furniture, table utensils, coins, tavern-tokens, counters, hornbooks, ring-dials, an astrolabe, pomanders, posy rings, memorial rings, table-books, hour glasses, and the like. Few objects associated with the domestic economy of the age have been neglected, and fewer still of those specifically alluded to in the plays.

So far we have confined our survey to books, manuscripts, and other material dating from the sixteenth and seventeenth centuries. But Mr. Folger did not, in his enthusiasm for the old, make the mistake of limiting himself to early material; he gathered also material bearing on the poet's later influence on the culture and thought of the world; and, further, he added the scholarly apparatus needed adequately to equip his collections for research.

In accordance with this ideal conception of a library, he sought to bring together all the modern editions of Shakespeare both in English and in foreign languages. Of the collected works he gathered (counting duplicates, many having a special value) more than a thousand editions; and of the individual plays—including "practically all the seventeenth- and eighteenth-century adaptations"—an equally remarkable number; for example, *Hamlet* in upwards of eight hundred editions. With the same zeal he assembled modern critical studies—books, pamphlets, dissertations, magazine articles, even newspaper-clippings—bearing on the dramatist and his contemporaries. About the more eminent Shakespearian scholars he formed special collections that serve not only to memorialize them, but to enrich and illuminate their published work. J. O. Halliwell-Phillipps, for instance, is represented by nearly a thousand autograph letters, mainly relating to scholarly matters, and by over six hundred other items listed under his name. Malone, Steevens, Collier, Fleay, Furnivall, and others are honored in similar fashion. Even the notorious forger Ireland is given "proud eminence" in a remarkable collection of his fabrications.

The history of Shakespeare on the stage is revealed in (besides the ordinary published treatises): almost a quarter of a million play-bills; manuscript accounts and records of various theaters; prompt-books, as used by Garrick, Kemble, Booth, the Keans, Macready, Faucit, Phelps, Irving, Robertson, etc.; thousands of letters by or about distinguished actors; diaries, memoirs, and journals of persons associated with the theater; portraits of eminent players as they appeared in actual life or in famous rôles; prints and photographs illustrating well-known performances; stage-properties, costumes, and scenic designs; and miscellaneous other material directly or indirectly of value for students of the subject. About individual actors, naturally, Mr. Folger tended to form special collections. The most extensive is that relating to David Garrick, consisting of several thousand items, such as: ten oil-portraits (including three by Sir Joshua Reynolds); over one hundred original manuscripts of prologues, epilogues, and poems in Garrick's autograph; approximately four hundred autograph letters; scores of personal relics (for example, his journal, note-book, marriage-certificate, memorial ring, silver table-service, death-mask); and numerous letters, prints, curios, books, manuscripts, pamphlets, newspaper-clippings, and the like, concerning his life and stage-career.

Shakespeare's influence on "the great ones" of the world is revealed in an astonishing collection of association-copies of his works, many of which are enriched with manuscript annotations. The list includes most of the subsequent English men of letters, as Killigrew, Dryden, Pope, Burns, Gray, Lamb, Scott, Coleridge, George Eliot, Thackeray, Shelley, Carlyle, Ruskin, Browning, Tennyson, Shaw; most of the eminent actors, as Garrick, Booth, Sarah Siddons, Charlotte Cushman, Irving, Ellen Terry, Tree, Kean, Macready; virtually all the important editors of Shakespeare, as Theobald, Pope, Warburton, Capell, Chalmers, Steevens, Johnson, Malone, Collier, Furness; famous American statesmen and writers, as Washington, John Adams, Lincoln, Hawthorne, Lowell, Holmes, Taylor, Whitman, Field; members of royalty, as Queen Elizabeth of Bohemia, King Louis XVI, King William IV, King George IV, Queen Victoria, Napoleon III; and persons of miscellaneous claims to distinction, as Madame de Pompadour, Ignatius Donnelly (his copy "filled with his cryptograms"), Thomas Nast, Francis Burnand (the editor of *Punch*), and General Tom Thumb. The total number of association-copies runs into several hundred. Besides their purely sentimental interest, they contain much that is illuminating as to the effect produced by the poet on varied minds, and much that is of real value for an understanding of the plays.

Shakespeare's influence in the field of the graphic and sculptural arts is exemplified by collections of paintings (by Lawrence, Gainsborough, Reynolds, Blake, Turner, Cruikshank, West, Peters, Opie, Stothard, Sully, Kauffmann, Hamilton, etc.), statues (by Roubiliac, Story, Mélingue, Carrier-Belleuse, Ward, MacMonnies, etc.), busts, carvings, miniatures, medallions, original drawings, water colors, mezzotints, porcelain figures, and prints of various kinds. Of prints alone there are perhaps fifty thousand; of oil-paintings, over two hundred.

Finally, in order to provide the scholarly apparatus that is needed by those who seek to explore the unknown elements in Shakespeare's life, writings, and influence, Mr. Folger assembled dictionaries, bibliographies, concordances, glossaries, encyclopædias, technical periodicals, publications of learned societies, and all that vast body of reference material which is indispensable to research.

The Library is thus comprehensive, well-proportioned, and fully equipped for study. As an educational institution open to every one who is qualified to use its treasures, it should be a vital force in the cultural development of America. Further, beautifully housed in the building designed by Mr. Cret, it forms a wonderful memorial to the poet, of whom Emerson wrote, in words chosen by Mr. Folger to be carved over the great fireplace in the Reading Room:

> England's genius filled all measure
> Of heart and soul, of strength and pleasure,
> Gave to the mind its Emperor,
> And life was larger than before:
> Nor sequent centuries could hit
> Orbit and sum of Shakespeare's wit.
> The men who lived with him became
> Poets, for the air was fame.

THE BUILDING

BY

PAUL PHILIPPE CRET

THE BUILDING

IT MAY seem unnecessary verbally to describe the building which in this volume is so amply illustrated by drawings and photographs. Further, the impressions of any building which one person gains may be at wide variance with those of another observer; and if he happens to be also, as is now the case, the architect of that building, his judgment may well be suspected of partiality. However, an architectural work has two aspects: artistic, in its plastic and general dispositions; utilitarian, in its solution of definite problems imposed by the client. If comments on its merits may savor of apology or of boasting, information regarding the requirements which had to be met is needed for a proper understanding of its various details. The following notes, therefore, are what is expected of a guide book—a bald description, and not an appreciation.

One feature should be explained at the outset, since it has proved troublesome to those who, holding with good reason that the interior and exterior treatment of a building must possess unity, have wondered why the architecture of the façades is at such variance with the somewhat archæological character of the rooms. The reason is quite simple. Mr. and Mrs. Folger desired to see specimens of their collections displayed in a gallery recalling the period rooms of our museums, and, further, they thought that the scholars who were to work in the Library would feel most at home in surroundings reminiscent of the England of the XVIth or XVIIth centuries. On the other hand, the architect and the consulting architect could readily see that the site selected, facing a wide and straight avenue of one of the most classical of cities, surrounded by classical buildings and lying in the very shadow of the classical dome of the Capitol itself, would be inappropriate for an Elizabethan building. The early renaissance architecture of England which harmonizes so well with the winding streets of Oxford, or the picturesque landscape of countryseats, would be quite out of place in Washington, and the Library, if renaissance in type, would clash with its immediate neighbors, the Library of Congress and the Supreme Court building. It was therefore agreed that the architect should have full freedom in designing the exterior to harmonize with its surroundings, while making the interiors derive their inspiration from Shakespeare's England.

This point settled, the problem was to provide for the housing of (1) a world-famous library, (2) collections of painting, sculpture, and curios, constituting a small museum, and (3) a small theater to be used for the presentation of Shakespeare's plays in their original staging, and for lectures or concerts. Accordingly the following division in three distinct sections was adopted:

A.   The library, with a main reading room surrounded by open shelves and vaults for the most precious books and manuscripts; individual study rooms; stack rooms with allowance for future growth; a catalogue room; offices for the Director, Supervisor of Research, Superintendent, clerical staff, and cataloguers; a receiving room; a binding and repair room; and a photographic laboratory.

B.   The exhibition gallery, open to all visitors, and to be used for the display of paintings, sculpture, books and manuscripts, musical instruments, costumes, etc., with an entrance lobby and coat room; and reserve galleries for prints, paintings, etc.

C.   The theater, a reconstruction of a Shakespearian playhouse, with dressing-rooms, property-rooms, a lounge for the public, and a separate entrance vestibule.

Group A has been placed at the rear of the building in order that it might be protected from street noise, with the offices along Second Street; Group B, on East Capitol Street, where it is readily accessible to the public; Group C, on the Third Street front.

Besides these various units, provisions have been made for a Founders' suite, to be used by the governing board. There are also service rooms, a power plant for heating, ventilation, air-conditioning of the stacks and vaults, and, finally, ample storage space.

As seen from the street, the north façade of the building is preceded by a broad terrace and lawn, with the entrance to the exhibition gallery at the right end, and to the theater at the left end. Between these two entrances are the high windows of the exhibition room. The design of the façade can be said to center in a set of nine panel-reliefs depicting scenes in famous plays of Shakespeare—*A Midsummer Night's Dream, Romeo and Juliet, The Merchant of Venice, Macbeth, Julius Caesar, King Lear, Richard the Third, Hamlet,* and *King Henry IV*. These panels are the work of John Gregory, and the interest in them shown by visitors is testimony to their merit. The sculptor has obtained an intimate union of sculpture with architecture, a thing seldom achieved. Intelligible to all, his characterizations are nevertheless plastic, and avoid the pitfall of anecdotal sculpture. Through their own merit, and through their unusual location near the level of the eye instead of, as is customary, near the entablature of the building, these panel-reliefs successfully answer one of the wishes of Mr. Folger in reminding the passer-by of the beauty awaiting him in Shakespeare's work.

The two doors are flanked by reliefs of Pegasus, the symbol of lyric poetry, and are crowned with the masks of Tragedy and Comedy.

The attic has no ornamentation other than quotations, selected by Mr. Folger, which tell the poet's glory better than wreaths or festoons.

On Second Street, the windows of the administration group open on a garden, and a beautiful fountain with a graceful figure of Puck, modeled by Brenda Putnam. On Third Street, the walls of the theater are broken only by an exit-door and its steps. The service yard, on the south, allows direct access to the basement by delivery wagons. All the outside walls are of white Georgia marble.

The façades have been designed without thought either of precedent or of obedience to passing fashions, in anticipation, it seems, of what Royal Cortissoz recently stated in a review of the Folger Library: "Modernism does not need to be a formula any more than tradition needs to be such. It may be, instead, a state of mind, out of which beauty may emerge if the passion for beauty be there."

From the west vestibule, the exhibition rooms are entered on the left, while the administration officers and qualified readers use the corridor facing the entrance. The exhibition gallery is a paneled hall 22′ x 130′ and 30′6″ high, with a ceiling of all-over strap-work in low relief. The oak paneling gives a warm background for the oil paintings and the glass cases. In the center of the room a bust of the founder by John Gregory greets the visitors. The floor of Enfield tiles brings in the leitmotif of the building, the titles of Shakespeare's most famous plays. The two main doors of the gallery are surmounted by the arms of the United States and of Elizabeth's England respectively, while two minor doors of leaded glass allow a clear view of the reading room without interfering with the quiet needed by scholars working there. An indirect system of lighting has been devised which does not by its modernity clash with the traditional surroundings.

Through the eastern end of the gallery, the public reaches the theater lobby, which, like the west entrance, is a vaulted hall of Lorraine stone and rough plaster, with flagstone flooring. Here are found the coat rooms, and stairs to the theater gallery and to the public lounge in the basement. From the lobby, the theater proper is entered through a door surmounted by a relief showing children acting in a masque, inspired by an old wood carving. To make the theater as nearly as possible a reconstruction of a theater of Shakespeare's time, presented several problems. For one thing, it had to be of rather limited size, since it is more in the nature of a lecture room than of a regular theater comparable to the Swan, Globe, or Fortune; for another thing, some characteristic features of the old playhouses had to be discarded, such as the open-air pit where the public was left standing, and the window-openings on the outside, which, when daylight performances were the rule, were of no great consequence but became a hindrance to an artificially lighted stage. Above all, there was a dearth of information at our service. No graphic data is available, and the textual reference easily lead to architectural monstrosities, principally because they allude to playhouses of widely different types. This explains why the reconstructions and models proposed by many scholars are at odds with one another, and present so many absurd features when analyzed from the architectural point of view. The vagueness of actual data is usually supplemented by a superabundance of personal interpretations vitiated by an inadequate knowledge of contemporary architecture. Early it was seen that no reconstruction of a particular playhouse was possible or advisable, and that the aim ought to be to place the spectators in an atmosphere removed from later-day theatrical devices, and provide for the players a simple Elizabethan stage. To achieve this we had at our service the old inn courtyards with superimposed balconies leading to the guest rooms, evidently one of the sources of theater architecture in England. Further, from the contract of the Fortune theater, 1600, the disposition of the interior could be approximately achieved. The walls, as we are told, were made of "frame, lime, lath, and hair," the shadow was tile-covered, the posts were "square and wrought pilasterwise with carved proportions called satyrs"; and, finally, large use was made of bright painting to embellish the homely construction.

This is what the Folger Library's theater shows to the public, with the addition of modern stage lighting, the use of which is left to the discretion of stage directors.

The principal function of the Library is to facilitate study by Shakespearian scholars. The reading room, in spite of its size, due to the unusual development of the open shelves, had to retain the character of a private library. The original collection comprised 90,000 volumes; but provision had to be made for an ultimate capacity of 150,000 volumes without including the prints, water colors, playbills, photographs, and manuscripts. The reading room is entered from the administration corridor through the catalogue room. It is a typical English hall, with a high trussed roof, and lighted by three bay windows. Measuring 38′ x 131′, and 32′ high, it has two tiers of shelves, the usual stairs leading into the stacks, and electric book-lifts; and, for the most precious material, two large vaults accommodating 18,000 volumes, and two smaller vaults, all opening on the reading room floor. At the western end, the founder wished to have a reproduction of the apse window of Trinity Church at Stratford-on-Avon. For the modern stained glass of the original has been substituted stained glass developing the theme of the "Seven Ages of Man" from *As You Like It*. At the east end, a hall screen has for its central feature a reproduction of the Shakespeare Memorial in the same church, appropriately flanked by the portraits of the donors. Of the stacks below the reading room, little can be said except that they conform to the best type evolved in this country.

The private study rooms, photographic laboratory, space for reserve collections, and cataloguer's room, are distributed in the four stories of the building.

The Founders' suite, adjoining the administrative offices, contains a rich collection of antique furniture, carpets, tapestries, and mementoes of the founders.

The building measures 226′ x 111′ on a property 364′ x 186′. Its construction started in November 1929, and its dedication was held in April 1932.

In a letter to Mrs. Folger, the architect, remembering the conferences in which the plans of the building took shape and the early stages of its construction, wrote: "Every collaborator who came then or later in contact with Mr. Folger, was won by his faith in the enduring value of beauty. I never found a more harmonious group than that assembled for this undertaking—artists, administrators, builders."

To these men, the writer of this essay, and his partner, William H. Livingston, acknowledge again their indebtedness, and particularly to Mr. Alexander B. Trowbridge, the Consulting Architect, Mr. William Adams Slade, the Director, and the artists and craftsmen, their collaborators.

THE CONSTRUCTION
OF THE FOLGER SHAKESPEARE LIBRARY
WAS STARTED ON NOVEMBER 8, 1929

THE BUILDING WAS DEDICATED ON APRIL 23, 1932
THE ANNIVERSARY OF THE DEATH OF THE POET
THE CEREMONY BEING ATTENDED BY THE
PRESIDENT OF THE UNITED STATES
AND MANY OTHER DISTINGUISHED
GUESTS

∴

PAUL PHILIPPE CRET
Architect

ALEXANDER B. TROWBRIDGE
Consulting Architect

THE ARCHITECT ACKNOWLEDGES THE VALUABLE COLLABORATION OF

WM. H. LIVINGSTON, HIS PARTNER IN CHARGE OF THE PROJECT
GRAVELL & DUNCAN, CONSULTING STRUCTURAL ENGINEERS
ISAAC HATHAWAY FRANCIS, CONSULTING MECHANICAL ENGINEER
JOHN GREGORY, SCULPTOR OF THE SHAKESPEARE RELIEFS
BRENDA PUTNAM, SCULPTOR OF THE PUCK FOUNTAIN
AUSTIN PURVES, FOR THE PAINTED DECORATION
J. MONROE HEWLETT, FOR THE THEATER CURTAIN DECORATION
JOSEPH H. DULLES ALLEN, FOR THE TILE WORK
V. F. VON LOSBERG, FOR THE LIGHTING APPARATUS
J. HOPKINSON EVANS, FOR THE FURNITURE AND FURNISHINGS
NICOLA D'ASCENZO, FOR THE STAINED GLASS IN THE READING ROOM

THE BUILDERS WERE THE JAMES BAIRD COMPANY

∴

THE ADVICE AND SUGGESTIONS OF

MR. AND MRS. HENRY CLAY FOLGER
THE FOUNDERS OF THE LIBRARY

HERBERT PUTNAM
LIBRARIAN OF CONGRESS

WILLIAM ADAMS SLADE
DIRECTOR OF THE FOLGER SHAKESPEARE LIBRARY

JOSEPH QUINCY ADAMS
SHAKESPEARIAN SCHOLAR

WERE OF THE GREATEST VALUE DURING THE PREPARATION OF THE PLANS
AND THE CONSTRUCTION

LIST OF PLATES

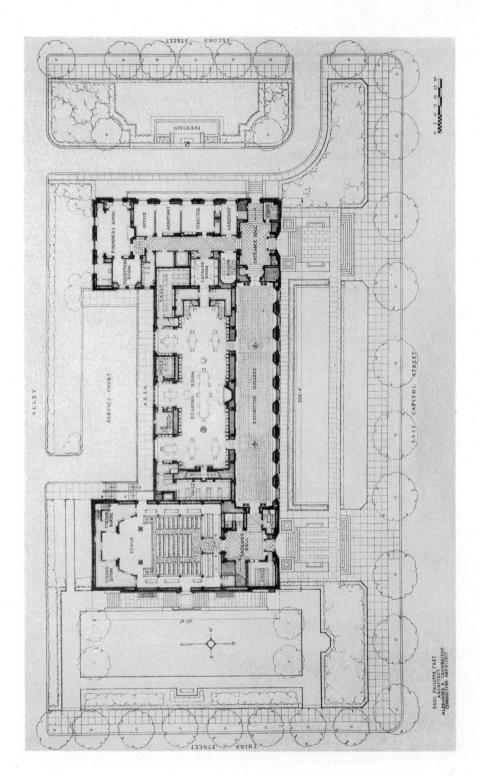

1. *Main floor plan*

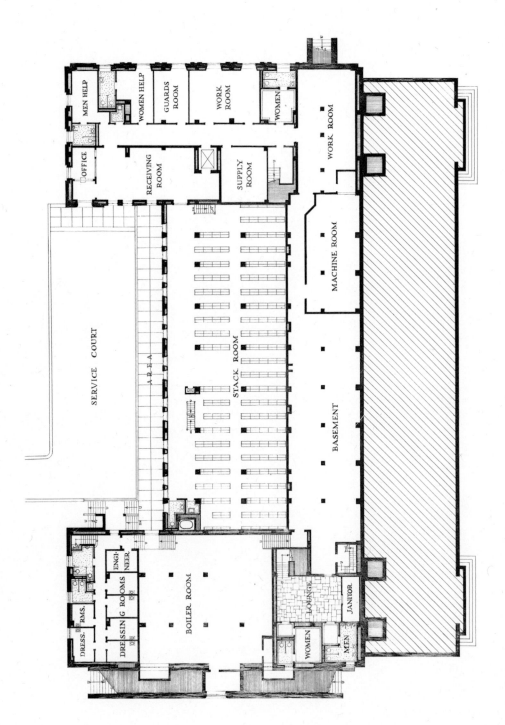

PAUL PHILIPPE CRET
ARCHITECT
ALEXANDER B. TROWBRIDGE
CONSULTING ARCHITECT

2.   *Ground floor plan, showing the book stack and services*

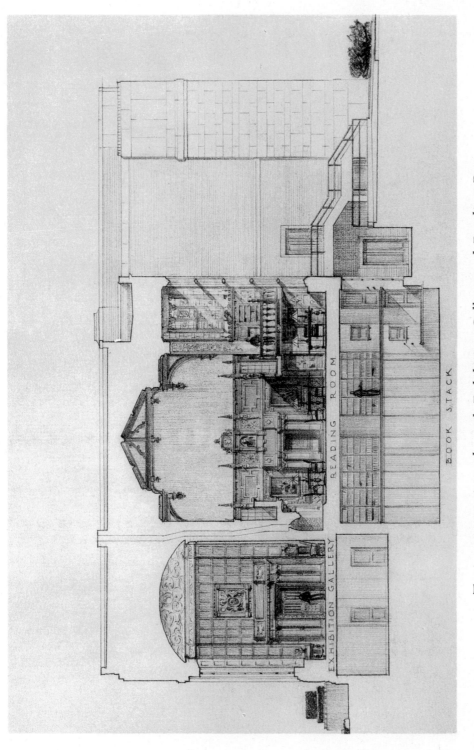

3. *Transverse section, through Exhibition Gallery and Reading Room*

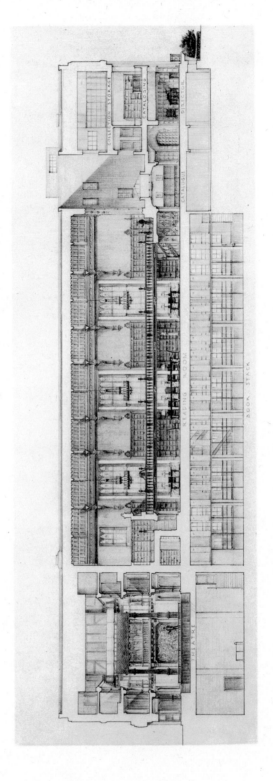

4. *Longitudinal section, through Theater, Reading Room, and administrative offices*

5. *The Library from East Capitol Street, showing the terrace, the entrances, and the windows of the Exhibition Hall*

6. *A detail of the façade, showing the nine reliefs by John Gregory*

7. *The Second Street façade. This portion of the building houses the administrative offices*

8. *Detail of one of the entrances on East Capitol Street*

9.   *Detail, main façade. The John Gregory relief of "The Tragedie of Julius Caesar," Act III, Scene* I

10.   *One of the terrace benches at the main entrance*

11. *Detail of balcony, façade on Second Street. The heraldic arms are those of Shakespeare*

12. *Theater exit on Third Street façade. The masks of Comedy and Tragedy, and dates of Shakespeare's birth and death*

THE TRAGEDIE OF KING LEAR

13. *The relief by John Gregory of "The Tragedie of King Lear,"*
Act III, Scene 2

THE MERCHANT OF VENICE

14.   *The relief by John Gregory of "The Merchant of Venice,"*
Act IV, Scene 1

THE TRAGEDIE OF MACBETH

15. *The relief by John Gregory of "The Tragedie of Macbeth,"*
Act IV, Scene 1

16. *The fountain on the west front. Figure of Puck by Brenda Putnam*
"Lord, what fooles these mortals be!" *—A Midsummer Night's Dream*

17. *The west entrance vestibule. Doorway to the administrative offices and steps to carriage entrance*

18. *Looking into the west entrance vestibule from the Exhibition Hall*

19. *The Exhibition Hall, general view*

20. *Exhibition Hall, detail*

here is not anything of human trial
hat ever love deplored or sorrow knew
o glad fulfilment and no sad denial
eyond the pictured truth that Shakespeare drew
William Winter

21. *Woodwork in the Exhibition Hall. The coat of arms of the
United States*

22.   *Exhibition Hall, detail of floor*

23. *The Reading Room, general view*

24.   *The end of the Reading Room. Window of the Seven Ages of Man*
by the D'Ascenzo Studios

25. *The Reading Room from the balcony*

26. *The Memorial screen in the Reading Room, with the Stratford-on-Avon Monument and the Salisbury portraits of Mr. and Mrs. Folger*

ENGLANDS GENIVS FILLED ALL MEASVRE
OF HEART AND SOVL OF STRENGTH AND PLEASVRE
GAVE TO THE MIND ITS EMPEROR,
AND LIFE WAS LARGER THAN BEFORE.
YOR SEQVENT CENTVRIES COVLD HIT
ORBIT AND SVN OF SHAKESPEARE'S WIT
THE MEN WHO LIVED WITH HIM BECAME
POETS FOR THE AIR WAS FAME

RALPH WALDO EMERSON

27.   *The great fireplace in the Reading Room, with Mrs. Folger*
standing at the left

28. *East entrance, Theater foyer and stairs to the gallery*

29. *The Stage of the Shakespeare Theater, showing the outer stage, inner stage, and upper stage*

30.   *The Theater, looking toward the entrance*

31. *Detail of the stage*

32.   *Side gallery of the Theater*

33. *The Founders' Room*

34. *The Director's office*

35. *The Catalogue Room, looking into the Reading Room*

36.   *The stairway, administration wing*